Blending a Family Successfully

Jeanette Moore

NEWMAN SPRINGS PUBLISHING
320 Broad Street
Red Bank, NJ 07701

First originally published by Newman Springs Publishing 2024

ISBN 979-8-89061-838-2 (Paperback)
ISBN 979-8-89061-839-9 (Digital)

Printed in the United States of America

This book is dedicated, first, to my Heavenly Father, in the precious name of my Lord and Savior Jesus Christ, through the help and inspiration of Holy Spirit for giving me the courage and opportunity to utilize my gift of writing. Having been married twice, and thereby experienced the ups and downs of blending a family twice in my lifetime, through the grace of God, has shaped and molded me to give an account of my experiences. Giving birth to this book resulted from those experiences of which Godly wisdom was imparted unto me to share with the world on how to blend a successful family. I would be remiss if I failed to mention my two spouses (who are deceased), children, grandchildren, and countless family and friends.

Contents

Preface...vii

Introduction...ix

1   Faith 1

2   Expectations...3

3   Core Values...7

4   Parenting Styles..9

5   Counseling...12

6   Leveling Up 16

7   Bridging the Gap 20

8   Finances..23

9   Effective Discipline 26

10   Communication 30

11   A Firm Foundation 33

12   Conclusion 40

Acknowledgments 43

Appendix: Pew Research Report Statistics............45

Preface

My goal in writing *Blending a Family Successfully* is to encourage nuclear families: widowed and single parents with children; caregivers for the elderly (parents and grandparents); as well as caregivers for adopted, fostered, and orphaned children. Whatever situation or circumstance that brings about blending a family, know that in order to have a strong family unit, the process is much bigger than the perfect picture that is painted. Without faith, love, trust, and patience, the family unit will suffer; and the foundation will be shaken. But know there is hope by giving thought to the necessary steps written in this book that will guide you through the process of successfully achieving better outcomes and thus building a strong family unit!

Introduction

Nuclear families are growing continuously every day. The traditional family has, for some time, become few wherein the picture-perfect family structure no longer exists. Nuclear families have now become the "new wave" family structure of this generation and the generations to come. With so many facets in the family structure that have developed over the years and what it looks like today, problems have arisen in how to successfully blend a family, such as socioeconomic factors, cultural differences, prejudices, psychological behaviors, and more. Giving thought to the necessary steps written in this book and applying them will change the trajectory of how a family is to be blended. It will also give insight for a positive start as you navigate through the process, especially in areas that need to be fine-tuned and adjusted. The stories in this book are true accounts of nonfictional characters so as to preserve the integrity of this book while still protecting the privacy of those who have shared some of their shortcomings, insights, inadequacies, and disappointments in blending a family successfully. This God-inspired book will give ease to the problematic situations that will challenge the moral fabric of a family that is blending to become a successful family unit!

And if a house is divided against itself,
that house will not be able to stand.

—Mark 3:25 (ESV)

CHAPTER 1

Faith

The Bible's definition of *faith*: "*Now faith is the assurance of things hoped for, the conviction of things not seen*" (Hebrew 11:1 ESV). What does your faith look like when you see the future with a mate and his/her children besides your own? Do you have the assurance that everything will work out because you have hope in the relationship? Or do you hope, knowing that blending a family is in God's foreordained will for your life, and take a leap of faith to go through the process? These are some very valid questions to ponder about why faith is so important, as it gives hope in every situation and/or circumstance we find ourselves in and to be able to walk this path of life, knowing that everything will work out for the good of everyone involved. It takes faith to believe that your prayers will be answered when you are in the midst of blending a successful family unit. Whatever your faith looks like (big or small) in relationship to your religion and/or belief system, it helps to know that God is invested in your home, family, and plans.

It will give you hope and lead you to achieve positive outcomes throughout the process of blending a family. Yes, along the way, there will be obstacles that will try to take you off course, but in keeping the faith, you will not lose your footing. It will bring you back into alignment that all things in the process are working together for the good of the entire family unit.

> And we know that for those who love God all things work together for good, for those who are called according to his purpose. (Romans 8:28 ESV)

Charles and Claire had to have known through their believing faith that they could blend their families successfully, even when they were still unaware of their expectations and had some unclear choices. They pushed forward in spite of the obstacles and challenges that came along the way, hoping that their families would become the family God intended for it to be: a successful family unit.

> Now faith is the assurance of things hoped for, the conviction of things not seen. (Hebrews 11:1 ESV)

CHAPTER 2

Expectations

During their dating process, Charles and Claire chose not to involve their children until they felt the time was right, which was after their engagement. During their courtship, they never had a conversation as to what their expectations were in blending their families. They were raising their children to the best of their abilities, not keeping in mind their differing parenting styles. They were raising their children from two perspectives: Charles was more permissive, and Claire, more authoritative. Charles had three young children at the time (Sandra, ten; Mike, eight; and Junior, six) and Claire had two children of her own (Danny, twelve, and Millie, nine).

Before blending a family, you need to ask yourself or give thought to the following questions:

1. *Will I be a better parent toward my stepchildren as I am with my own?*

    This will always pose a challenge as children will have a difficult time adjusting to any other authoritative figure that they are not accustomed to. (For younger children, the adjustment is not as complicated though.) This will put a strain on the new parent in the beginning, but it will get better as the family makes the adjustments.

2. *If any adjustments are to be made, can they be made without any partiality?*

    Both parents need to be transparent enough to work on any partiality issues when it comes to their own and make sure to level the playing field so as to resolve any insecurity that may arise among the children and thus avoid unwanted character flaws and misunderstandings.

3. *Will I be willing to love past rejection?*

    Rejection is one of the toughest character flaws to get rid of especially when it is the injured party that is making the adjustment. It can be best overcome when you can look at the situation and understand that change can bring about feelings of doubt, worry, and fear. Know also that our loving God is able to grace you with peace and comfort and that patience will have its perfect work as the family transitions into getting to know each other better.

4. *Will I not compare myself to the parents of my stepchildren that are absent from their lives?*

    A parent can never model themselves into the absent parent of a stepchild(ren).

You need to be your own authentic self in becoming the role model and parent the child(ren) need and be able to complement the other parent's parenting style. This will build a foundation that is based on love within the home.

5. *Will I be willing to put the work in strengthening our family unit?*

Without it, you will not have the firm foundation you are hoping for. The family will not hold up. You have to be willing to put the work in to have a successful family unit. It will take prayer, patience, and love to arrive at the end result, which is a healthy and loving home. Everyone has a part to play, even the children.

6. *What will our faith structure look like as a family if we have differing faiths?*

Having differing faiths can complicate things in the beginning. This is an area that needs to be discussed beforehand to eliminate the frustration of having to involve the child(ren). The family unit will become disjointed and won't come to be in one accord with regard to the morals and principles that the parents have set for the children. Parents need to decide which faith will give them the best results in rearing their children in the admonition of the Lord.

These are some of the important questions both parents should give thought to before blending a family. Charles and Claire did not have this conversation or even ask themselves any of the above questions. Had they done so, they would have had better insight and understanding as to what it would look like when they blend their families together.

> For I know the plans I have
> for you, declares the LORD, plans
> for welfare and not for evil, to
> give you a future and a hope.
> (Jeremiah 29:11 ESV)

CHAPTER 3

Core Values

What are core values? Core values are beliefs that you and your partner fundamentally desire to see established within the family structure to help the family navigate through life's challenges with a goal (or several goals) in mind. Core values should be the brand in which the family is striving to achieve and the fulfillment of those achievements. God honors the family structure, and His desire is to see that the family is faithfully guided by (1) love to endure all things; (2) faith to believe that goals and dreams will manifest and the reassurance that situations and circumstances will become better even though you do not see them; (3) trust in God as you navigate through the blending process; and (4) patience to wait and know that every situation and circumstance will work together for the good of the family in God's own time as you trust Him through the process.

The importance of having the core values of love, faith, trust, and patience in place will allow for a greater appreciation and expectation as you and your partner begin the blending process with your families. Your expectations will become clearer as it will give you a bigger picture of what your desired family structure will look like through discipline from the deposit of these core values in the home. As each partner mesh together differing parenting styles, having these core values of love, faith, trust, and patience in place will also set the tone for positive outcomes when blending your children's as well as that of the parents' personalities, strengths, weaknesses, and insecurities.

Parenting Styles

Parenting style plays a big part and is vitally important when it comes to blending a family. The other parent may embody a parenting style a lot different from the one that is being exhibited in the home on a daily basis. It also invites conflict to the point where the other parent would either have to submit, compromise, object, or become uninvolved. This is where the confusion begins, which changes the trajectory of the family structure.

Charles had a permissive/uninvolved parenting style, and Claire was more of an authoritative/authoritarian. You could tell the difference in the parenting style exhibited by the way their children react toward them as well as the behavior being shown by them and how they conduct themselves. There were times when Claire would become frustrated with Charles's children because of their lack of discipline. They did not have behavioral problems per se, but they exemplified "a behavior of entitlement" wherein if it was not their way, then it would be no way at all. On the other hand, Claire's children are more disciplined in acknowledging authority as they are aware of the consequences they would have to face if they acted in any disrespectful way toward Charles. For years, it was challenging and stressful for the both of them as Claire realized she could not change Charles's children's behavior toward her unless there were boundaries set in place. This would be contingent upon Charles having to be comfortable in confronting and willing to address his children's boundaries that would address their behavior and respect for Claire as they move forward to building a home that was more loving and trusting. Charles had not taken into account that one day his children would be put under a position of authority by another parent that had a different parenting style from him. Charles continued to parent them the way he was accustomed to, which allowed for emotional stress to continue on both sides as his children's behavior with Claire was far from improving.

In order to get the outcomes you are looking for, both sides are to make sure that the parenting styles would complement each parent as well as each child. They must be conducive for all so as to bring about harmony within the family. This is essential along with prayer. Prayer is the key while faith unlocks the door and gives you the support that will help the family through the blending process. Not only does prayer unleashes faith, but prayer also unleashes wisdom and the insight to better understand problems and situations that may arise, helping you navigate through them when they surface.

> Blessed is the one who finds wisdom, and the one who gets understanding. (Proverbs 3:13)

CHAPTER 5

Counseling

Charles and Claire were destined to be joined in holy matrimony together with the hope of blending their families. They dated for several months and decided to get married. During the engagement process, Charles and Claire decided not to involve their children in marital counseling as they did not know which direction they were going to be led. The children suspected that they were becoming close as they were spending more time together and were involving them on occasions in various family activities. Charles proposed to Claire, and they became engaged. During the engagement, they gradually interacted more with the children, going out to dinner, attending sports events, as well as community and church events. Everything appeared to be going well, although Claire did not feel the love being demonstrated from Charles's children, outside of the fact they were always cordial to her. Claire knew the children were appeasing their dad by fronting a better behavior in his presence, and at the same time, they were unhappy with her. On occasion, Claire would ask Charles how the children felt about the engagement and her soon becoming their stepmom. He would assure her every time that everything was fine, but Claire knew deep down that it was not. Claire continued on with that of having a committed heart willing to love his children unconditionally despite the odds and, by the grace of God, hoped things would change for the better. Claire loved Charles and his children and was willing to put in the work as if they were her own children in order to move forward with their plans for marriage.

The defining moment came when it was time to go through premarital counseling and the minister acknowledged to Charles and Claire that the children were welcome to join in the counseling sessions if they felt comfortable involving them. Claire was surprised and elated that the children were involved in the sessions, as it would put her mind at ease as they move forward with the marriage plans. But Charles felt that it would not be a good idea to involve the children as they would not understand a lot of what will be discussed. He thought that there might be questions that may make them feel uncomfortable; therefore, he opted out to not have his children get involved in the counseling process. So since Charles was not willing to have his children get involved in the counseling sessions, Claire also chose not to have her children participate. Claire was very disappointed with Charles's decision, and the reasons for his decision left Claire with concerns as they progressed along with their marriage plans. Not having the closure and support from Charles, which she needed, would have given her a clearer picture of what it was she was working with and give her a better insight as to how she and Charles were going to handle whatever concerns the children might have about their father being engaged to be married. Claire, not having Charles support, was left without closure regarding their children as to what she was discerning would not be clear for some time. Claire had to trust her heart and instincts and rely on the leading of Holy Spirit to get her to better understand her stepparent relationship role and better relate to the children as time went on. She decided that she was going to let love prevail and let its perfect work, work within the family as she moved forward with the marriage. The thought never escaped Claire as it became clear to her, being often reminded that having the children involved in premarital counseling would have given them better outcomes as a family unit.

Premarital counseling and/or any form of counseling is imperative to ease the concerns and insurmountable pressures that may arise both within the parents and the children. In many cases, the sessions are designed to have an impact on the problems and concerns of the family as it bring into account faith-based applications needed to assist them of the process. Going into counseling sessions will also release a sense of freedom spiritually, emotionally, and physically. It would put things into proper perspective for all involved. Being in the midst of a trusted person such as your pastor, a clinical counselor, teacher, mentor, or friend will make the children more comfortable in expressing their feelings of concern, doubts, and fears. This would help relieve them of any pressure(s) or anxiety that would cause them to feel contrary about their parents and/or new stepparents and vice versa.

> The plans of the heart belong to man, but the answer of the tongue is from the LORD. All the ways of a man are pure in his own eyes, but the LORD weighs the spirit. Commit your work to the LORD, and your plans will be established. (Proverbs 16:1–3 ESV)

CHAPTER 6

Leveling Up

What does it mean to level up? Leveling up is being true to yourself and your convictions. In order to bring the best you to the table, you have to realize and recognize that God will not have allowed you to be put into a situation or circumstance without giving you the ability and provision to be the "best version of you" in the process, without compromise or boundaries. Embracing your convictions and not compromising allows you to be transparent and open to the leading of Holy Spirit as He leads and guides you through every obstacle. But you have to be truthful with yourself that you are willing to put the work in order to get the results you are looking for, as you yield to the Holy Spirit's leading. Your convictions would allow you to know, or discern, that the problem may or may not be you. It would also make you more willing to make whatever allowances and/or changes to correct the problem(s) that resides within you. It would give you a clearer picture of the person you are and the person you need to become in order to be effective in your role as a parent and/or or guardian within the family. The work that is imperative for the parents is to become good stewards and witnesses in the home. This is done by the reading of God's word, being consistent in prayer, and becoming the parents God intend for you to be. You will be equipped, as you are being led and directed by Holy Spirit to seek the word of God for every situation, need, and circumstance as well as for direction as you journey to blend your family.

> Your word is a lamp to
> my feet and a light to my path.
> (Psalm 119:105 ESV)

Charles and Claire came from faith-based communities whereby their faiths and their relationship with God had been nurtured into their own individual level of convictions. They were challenged on several occasions to apply God's word with prayer. Blending a family can bring about a barrage of issues if you do not deal with the baggage resulting from previous relationships. It is important to identify what you are willing to leave behind and not bring into the relationship as it can be damaging to the family as it relates to insecurities, painful memories, etc. If those areas are not dealt with and continue to lie dormant and not brought up into the relationship, it will have a great impact on the freedom you have in the relationship. It will keep you in bondage to your past and rob you of the joys of your future and of becoming an effective parent.

Charles becoming a widow with three very young children left him in a state of bewilderment. He could not see his way nor be true to his convictions. He felt he had to protect and shield his children from pain and past hurts caused by him losing his wife and the children's mother. Experiencing such a devastating loss caused Charles to have an unhealthy view of life. He had become a recluse, and the children were sheltered, which had impacted their emotional and sociological state. Dealing with disillusionment as to how Charles was raising his children had caused Claire to become frustrated and angry. Charles felt he had to keep his children protected and shielded from the stresses and cares of life. This made it difficult for both Charles and Claire to coparent as Charles never allowed Claire to interact with authority unless it was carried out through him. Claire's standards did not change as her intentions for Charles and his children were good, but she did not realize that she was dealing with a stronghold from this past that needed to be broken. Through consistent prayer and fasting, Charles began to open up to Claire and share the hurt, pain, and frustration of losing a wife and having to raise three young children alone. Charles felt his life was caving under him and was under the doctor's care for clinical depression as a result of the trauma of experiencing the loss that had caused setbacks like having to give up his job to take care of his children. As a result, he lost everything including his home and had to pack up with his children to go live with his parents until he could get back on his feet. And by the grace of God, he was able to regroup and make a life for himself and his children up until he met Claire and they became husband and wife.

CHAPTER 7

Bridging the Gap

When blending a family, you are intertwining everyone's personalities in order to bring balance to the family structure. Children, when they are in the beginning stages of their tween and teen years, have already embodied character traits that can be contrary to your expectations as a stepparent. They have made up in their minds as to their position and how they would handle situations before they occur. They will let you know where you stand in their world as not being either the mother or father that is not present in the home. As a stepparent, you are put into a position of proving yourself time and time again to either appease or satisfy their position in the home. Both parents have to be prepared to meet everyone where they are and address any strengths, weaknesses, jealousies, or behaviors so as to bring about a respectful and unified home in spite of disparity in the parenting styles. The gap has to be bridged, so the children and the parents from both sides should reconcile and work through any differences and alleviate conflict and misunderstandings. It is also imperative that both parents' economic lifestyles are to be accounted so as to bring into balance what the children were accustomed before the family has begun to blend. Everyone should be on the same leveled playing field in order to keep the harmony, respect, and balance within the home.

> For jealousy makes a man furious, and he will not spare when he takes revenge. (Proverbs 6:34 ESV)

Charles and Claire were challenged by their children's jealous and insecure behavior. The children had started to become competitive toward one another as they, in comparing their differences, wanting be treated like the other. If one child notices that the other is being nurtured more on a repetitive basis or being shown more attention, it would cause resentment and animosity from the child. It had become stressful for Charles and Claire to the point that they had to acknowledge each child's insecurities and be able to manage them without causing any offense or disappointment. They had to make adjustments in the best interest of the children, which took time and patience. There were times Charles's children consulted with him without Claire being present, and like so, Claire's children would consult with her without Charles being present. It had become the norm in the home for years, even until the oldest child of

Claire (Danny) went off to college. The other children were getting older, and having started coming into their own individuality, they become more acquainted with each other's personalities and started to mesh well and accept each other's differences.

For years as they worked on bridging the gap. They learned to let patience have its perfect work in an effort to keep the family structure on a firm foundation! And it did!

> Come now, let us reason together, says the LORD: though your sins are like scarlet, they shall be as white as snow; though they are red like crimson, they shall become like wool. (Isaiah 1:18 ESV)

CHAPTER 8

Finances

Finances should never be overlooked when it comes to blending a family. According to statistics, one of the top reasons why divorces are on the rise is because of finances. When blending a family, depending on what the family economic situation looks like, finances will always play an important role in providing the family the freedom to enjoy a quality of life that will not put a strain on the family's progress. Everything costs when it comes to fulfilling a need within the family. Some of these financial needs are dependent upon the situation and circumstances of the family as a whole, such as tithing, child care, education, food, clothing, housing, medical, savings, transportation as well as other essential necessities. Each partner needs to sit down and discuss their financial situation so as to get a clearer picture of what it will look like when they combine their income together as well as discuss what financial adjustments that are needed to be made so as to keep the family in a positive, well-adjusted, and workable financial position. God promises according to Philippians 4:19 (ESV): *"And my God will supply every need of yours according to his riches in glory in Christ Jesus."* This promise is not only a reality and truth of God's Word, but it also carries with it the responsibility of stewardship in taking care of all that He has blessed and entrusted you with in order to live the quality of life you desire as well as rewarding you when you apply the principles and truths of His word to every area of life. A steward is one that manages and cares for something that is of usefulness, which best describes money and/or finances. Financial freedom comes when finances are cohesively managed by both parties in an amicable manner.

> And my God will supply every need of yours according to his riches in glory in Christ Jesus. (Philippians 4:19 ESV)

Charles and Claire, during their first year of marriage, had to deal with many financial obstacles because of Charles having being challenged by situations that were untimely and came at a bad time. It was the timing that caught them off guard, and they were not able to prevent the financial breakdown from happening or to prepare for it. Charles had become stagnant in a crisis that had him in a holding pattern. He was in the process of trying to secure his benefits from the US Army and Social Security from a disability claim he filed a few years prior to him meeting Claire. It was for an injury he sustained while serving in the Army. The process had taken months, and Claire had to pick up the slack, working tirelessly to keep things going. But the bills had started to pile up, and they fell behind their payments. Their bank accounts had dried up, and the mortgage payments also fell behind. It was impossible for the family to be sustained by one income, but they kept their faith in the midst of it all. God proved merciful in the midst of the process. When it looked like there was not hope and everything started to spiral, God mercifully stepped in and blessed Charles with a resolution to his disability claim. He received all his pending benefits along with back payments. This allowed them to manage their finances and come out from under the financial hardships they encountered.

Life happens. This is a sure reminder when discussing finances together. It will give a clearer picture and better outlook in forecasting how things will look down the road. Making the necessary adjustments together will give you a healthy financial outcome should a financial crisis happens. And also to become financially equipped and liberated, without having to experience financial and/or debt pitfalls. Having a healthy view of the family's finances by way of income and expense forecasting will give you a clearer picture of what is coming in and what is going out as well as what remains in excess to be used for future financial needs.

CHAPTER 9

Effective Discipline

During the first two years of family blending, Charles and Claire ran into a few stressful events in dealing with Charles's children and having to bring a workable solution to some of their behavior that Claire had to face, not being aware of them from the start of the relationship. It was now evident to Claire that the biggest mistake she and Charles made coming into the marriage was not involving the children in their premarital counseling sessions beforehand. Charles, being the protective loving father he was to his children, felt the need to protect his children's emotional stability, even at the cost of having to face the consequences later down the road in the marriage. Because of Charles's lack of support on Claire's behalf, Claire had become emotionally detached and exhausted when it came to addressing household chores that were not done when Claire delegated them to the children and other concerns such as cleaning their rooms and having to deal with their disrespectful attitudes when they were made to comply with doing the chores at their father's request. Charles had been the liaison for his children in getting them to do what was asked of them without addressing and/or reprimanding to do what Claire asked of them to do. Charles's mishandling and lack of support on Claire's behalf left her defenseless when it came to disciplining and gaining respect from his children. Claire realized that these behaviors were what they had been accustomed to after their mother passed, having been nurtured and coddled by their father. Claire also realized that the problem was with Charles and how he had parented his children. She knew that it will take time and patience for them to make whatever necessary adjustments in order to see things change.

When blending a family, both partners have to assess each of their children and where they are emotionally in the relationship. Each child brings to the table their own uniqueness, personality, insecurities, weaknesses, and strengths. Communication is vitally important as it is the vehicle that will open the door to the various issues of concern. In order to get the children all on the same level to receive from both parents, the parents should find out where they are in the relationship and in having to embrace a new family different from the one they were accustomed to. It takes time, patience, and understanding from both parents and/or partners in order to work through whatever situations they encounter with their children so it does not arouse any friction or jealousy with one another. It is vitally important that both partners take into account and address their parenting styles with each other so that they can come to a mutual understanding and agreement as what parenting style they would choose in disciplining their children. After settling into a parenting style, the parents will then become accountable in supporting each child without compromise or partiality as well as in supporting of each other. Both partners have to affirm the new disciplinary actions implemented within the family structure because it will then give the children a better insight into how they are to be disciplined as well as know what the repercussions will be. Knowing their parents' expectations will achieve better outcomes. In time, each child will become comfortable in making the necessary adjustments in leveling the playing field as they move forward in embracing changes to the family structure.

Children are resilient and will adjust to their environment when there is structure. Each child is unique and has their own specific needs that are to be addressed as they are being molded to fit the dynamics of parenting. This may take time and effort for them to adjust. Communication is the key in getting each child to be heard and their needs met within the home, having to endure the absence of the other parent that is no longer present in their lives. It will allow you to become more equipped and sensitive in dealing with each child's behavior and disciplinary outcomes.

You shall teach them diligently to your children, and shall talk of them when you sit in your house, and when you walk by the way, and when you lie down, and when you rise. (Deuteronomy 6:7 ESV)

CHAPTER 10

Communication

While blending a family, communication is vitally important and should always be open to everyone in the home. Without good communication, it will be impossible to weed out any problems, circumstances, and situations that may arise. Smartphones, smart televisions, and other smart devices have invaded the homes; whereby, communication has become more and more limited. As the technological AI world has taken over the homes, everyone is either being entertained or distracted by one, two, or three social-media platforms throughout the day. Children have become more fastened and pacified through their phones as communication within the home no longer has priority. Verbal communication will allow each person in the household to become more accountable in relating to each other and each other's needs and in becoming secure in navigating through their respective needs, goals, dreams, and visions of the family as a whole.

In the homes, there must be that expression of each person's emotions in order for each person to be relatable to one another. Without it, chaos and confusion will constantly arise, and this will open the door to other circumstances and situations that will keep the family contained and not free and/or liberated to work through those specific areas of concern, which will hinder the peace of God from being in the home. If the family structure is to survive and be strengthened, communication within the home must become a priority in order for everyone to gain knowledge and understanding of what each person's individual personalities and character bring to the family unit as well as their individual place of harmony as the family continue to blend and become more loving, nurtured, and well-grounded family unit.

Charles and Claire had to overcome a serious communication problem within their home as each one had to face opposition from each one of their children toward the other parent. It had become frustrating as Charles's children would never express their feelings to Claire, and Claire's children would not express their feelings with Charles. When it came to expressing their feelings, Charles's children would express their feelings to each other or with Charles and Claire's children would express their feelings only to Claire. In the beginning, the children were frustrated because Charles took the initiative to enforce the issue that his children refer to Claire as "Mom" and Claire's children refer to him as "Dad." The children were reluctant and continued calling Charles and Claire on a first-name basis. As time went on, this was an area that was not enforced or made a priority. Claire was determined to not let rejection of not being called "Mom" interfere with her relationship with Charles's children and remained faithful in mothering and nurturing the children without the discord of not addressing her as "Mom" come between them. Charles then decided that his children call Claire Ma, which was what her children affectionately addressed her on a regular basis. Eventually, the children started to open up more with each other, and then they started opening up to both Charles and Claire. Charles and Claire have become more in tuned and relatable with their children through maintaining better communication skills as well as expressing certain boundaries that the children were to be governed by as they were not accustomed to certain disciplines in the beginning of the marriage. It took time and patience; but communication became better between Charles, Claire, and their children as each one worked at becoming more accountable and relatable in their home.

> Let no corrupting talk come
> out of your mouths, but only
> such as is good for building up,
> as fits the occasion, that it may
> give grace to those who hear.
> (Ephesians 4:29 ESV)

CHAPTER 11

A Firm Foundation

What does it look like to have a firm foundation? A firm foundation is having a blended family that will overcome the challenges of life on every level, defying the odds of what makes a family a family. Blending a family brings with it joys and pains, as with any other family structure regardless of race, religion/creed, culture, tradition, status, sexual orientation, and lifestyle contentions. What makes family blending different and unique is the combining and bringing two families together in the making of one unit. Having to navigate through the obstacles of imperfection, personality differences, character flaws, behavior patterns, anger, confusion, pain, jealousy, and strife can bring about a stressful and relentless state of affairs to the family structure. Times have changed, and people are changing with the times wherein the traditional family model is becoming less prevalent today. Families are being comprised by many facets of family orientation when it comes to blending a family unit (i.e., caring for dependent parents/grandparents, caring for adopted or orphaned child(ren), stepparenting through marriage, and grandparents caring for their grandchildren to name a few). To begin the process it will take prayer, sacrifice, and commitment. But to blend a family successfully, it will take faith, love, trust, and patience.

Faith

Faith is a grace given by God to anyone who is willing to put their trust in Him in hoping for the impossible, even when there is no evidence and/or proof of manifestation aside from believing with expectancy. Hope is an anchor that is given to the soul of man and a rest to his spirit. It is the necessary component that encompasses the confidence and trust of each family member to bring into the family a more solid and hopeful reliance on God, in proof that the reality of an imperfect family unit can be made near perfect. Allowing faith to have its perfect work will challenge the family to take the necessary steps to seek God for direction, acknowledging every area of concern as the work is being put into action to rectify the problems as they are presented early on. Having faith is so endearing to God, as stated in Hebrews 11:6 (ESV): *"And without faith it is impossible to please him, for whoever would draw near to God, 'must believe that he exists' and that he rewards those who seek him."*

Love

Love that is exhibited in any family situation will in no doubt change the trajectory of the family relationship when problems surface. Love is an action word that shows commitment and allows for challenges and failures to arise in order for it to channel through the good as well as the bad. Love gives way to pain and afflictions; whereby, it should protect and cover each family member, making allowances for any mistakes and weaknesses without condemnation, but allowing edification to have its perfect work as it relates to any circumstances and situations that the family may encounter in order to lessen any conflicts or strongholds that may arise. Love never fails! It should be the precursor from the very start as the family is blending.

> For while we were still weak, at the right time Christ died for the ungodly. For one will scarcely die for a righteous person—though perhaps for a good person one would dare even to die—but God shows his love for us in that while we were still sinners, Christ died for us. (Romans 5:6–8 ESV)

Trust

Faith and love will embody trust. The family unit must have the trust factor working in each relationship within the family at all times. Without trust transcending throughout the family, the family will not survive the very foundation that it was built upon and fortitude that holds it together, which is love. Perfect love casts out fear. Having reliance upon one another such as we rely on God to handle any and all of our affairs is no different in having the same trust factor working within the family in knowing that each one is there for each other in an absolute dependable manner.

> For thus said the Lord God, the Holy One of Israel, "In returning and rest you shall be saved; in quietness and in trust shall be your strength." (Isaiah 30:15 ESV)

Patience

As with any family unit, it takes patience to stand the test of time, regardless of what is going on within the family in order to make whatever adjustments needed to bring resolve to any challenges that the family may encounter. For every problem there is a solution that needs to be weighed as well as tested and tried in order to bring peace and healing, without damaging the character and moral fabric of the family as a whole and for each individual family member. Time brings about change, and change produce results as patience is having her perfect work when the family is challenged with all kinds of obstacles and beset by human failures and weaknesses. God's grace and healing power are always at work through every situation that has been yielded to him throughout the process.

The family structure's firm foundation rests on the core values of faith, love, trust, and patience, which solidifies and embodies the presence of God working in and through every situation. As Christ is expressed in the home, His presence will be the light that illuminates every area of darkness. Christ should be the head in every home, and he is the light of the home that prepares the way.

> I therefore, a prisoner for the Lord, urge you to walk in a manner worthy of the calling to which you have been called, with all humility and gentleness, with patience, bearing with one another in love, eager to maintain the unity of the Spirit in the bond of peace. (Ephesians 4:1–3 ESV)

> If I speak in the tongues of men and of angels, but have not love, I am a noisy gong or a clang-

ing cymbal. And if I have prophetic powers, and understand all mysteries and all knowledge, and if I have all faith, so as to remove mountains, but have not love, I am nothing. If I give away all I have, and if I deliver up my body to be burned, but have not love, I gain nothing. Love is patient and kind; love does not envy or boast; it is not arrogant or rude. It does not insist on its own way; it is not irritable or resentful; it does not rejoice at wrongdoing, but rejoices with the truth. Love bears all things, believes all things, hopes all things, endures all things. Love never ends. As for prophecies, they will pass away; as for tongues, they will cease; as for knowledge, it will pass away. For we know in part and we prophesy in part, but when the perfect comes, the partial will pass away. When I was a child, I spoke like a child, I thought like a child, I reasoned like a child. When I became a man, I gave up childish ways. For now we see in a mirror dimly, but then face to face. Now I know in part; then

I shall know fully, even as I have been fully known. So now faith, hope, and love abide, these three; but the greatest of these is love. (1 Corinthians 13 ESV)

CHAPTER 12

Conclusion

Blending a family successfully can be challenging, but rewarding if the family is guided by the proper channels that will relieve any stressful events for each person in the family as they approach this challenge with faith, love, trust, courage, and respect. In blending a family successfully, the twelve fundamental steps outlined and discussed throughout this book will give you a good basis to start as you formulate and define your family structure that will give you the foundation that best describes your family's brand (core values) as you strive to understand your family as a whole as well as each individual person within the family. When blending a family, it is important not to forget that each person is unique, and he or she will add to the family in their own unique way as they relate to one another, understanding their boundaries and relating and respecting the boundaries of others. Challenges that may arise are there not to destroy the family structure but are there to allow God to work in the midst to bring peace, comfort, joy, and unity as the family navigates through their problems and circumstances in a healthy manner keeping in mind the four principles: faith, love, trust, and patience. Without these principles, the foundation will be and will remain fragile. Faith gives hope to the family; love will cover the family; trust will bind the family; and patience will guide the family through the hardships of life. Jesus, being the head of the home, gives expression to each one of these principles as they are carried out within the family structure while blending is taking place until the foundation becomes firm and pliable. God, who is the author and finisher of our faith, is the "banner" on which these four principles stand. As a believer, we can identify with each one of these principles as they are the expression of God's love and how He works in and through our lives. It takes faith to believe in the resurrected Christ; it took love to redeem mankind; it takes trust to know that He will provide and care for us; and patience to know His will is consistently at work in every situation and/or circumstance of our lives. I am reminded of a familiar hymn by Edward Mote (1834), *My Hope Is Built on Nothing Less*. A stanza of the hymn says, "*On Christ, the solid Rock, I stand; all other ground is sinking sand.*" In blending a family successfully, a firm foundation is having a home that is built on Christ, the solid Rock, and everything else will fall into place as a result of "victorious living!"

Everyone then who hears these words of mine and does them will be like "a wise man who built his house on the rock. (Matthew 7:24 ESV)

Acknowledgments

It is with heartfelt gratitude to the almighty God, who has equipped me with the gifts and talents not only to write this book but also to be obedient to His leading when He spoke to my heart to write; the Holy Spirit, who brought to my remembrance the things that I needed to know as it relates to my life experience blending a family; others who took the time to share their life experiences in blending a family while in the process of writing this book; and my Lord and Savior Jesus Christ, whose character I am influenced by as a role model in living this purpose-driven life.

I would like to thank my family and friends for believing in me and knowing that "nothing is impossible to him/her who believes!"

I can do all things through
Him who strengthens me.
(Philippians 4:13 ESV)

Pew Research Center Report: Prevalence of Blended Families

The following article is from a Pew Research Center Report written by Kristin Purcell, addressing the prevalence of blended families as the rise of two-parent households are becoming increasingly obsolete, leaving more families diversifying their family structures." Pew Research Center is a nonpartisan fact tank that informs the public about the issues, attitudes, and trends shaping the world. It conducts public opinion polling, demographic research, media content analysis, and other empirical social science research. Pew Research Center does not take policy positions. It is a subsidiary of <u>the Pew Charitable Trusts</u>.

While there aren't a lot of specific statistics on stepfamilies, Pew Research Center reports a generalized look at blended families in the US today. For the purpose of better understanding the blended family structure, a blended family is defined as any household that includes a stepparent, step-sibling, or half-sibling.

- Sixteen percent of children live in blended families.
- Per the US Bureau of Census, 1300 new stepfamilies are formed each day.
- 40% of families in the US are blended with at least one partner having a child from a previous relationship before marriage.
- The number of kids living in blended families has been stable for nearly thirty years.
- Children of Hispanic, Black, and White backgrounds are equally likely to live in this type of family.
- Children from Asian families are half as likely as Hispanic, Black, or white kids to be part of a blended family.
- Six in ten women's remarriages create blended families.

Statistics on Stepfamily Success

Every family is unique, and so is its success rate. However, stepfamily studies suggest about 60 to 70 percent of marriages involving children from a previous marriage fail, a statistic reiterated by the Census Bureau, which found that divorce increases in relation to the number of times one marries. This is about twice the percentage of overall marriages ending in divorce, which sits around 30–35 percent.

Part of what helps some stepfamilies be more successful rests on the children's perceived bonds with both parents inside the home. Adolescents who believe they have strong bonds with both their own mother and their stepfather in this type of family feel a greater sense of family belonging than kids who don't view both of these household relationships in a positive light.

Recent research from the UK found that kids from stable homes with different types of family structures were equally successful academically because of their family stability, not their family type. Thus, establishing a positive environment is more important than family type. What can make blended families work is having two cooperative parents, who create a stable, loving environment for their children.

Every Blended Family Is Unique

Because blended families appear to still be in the minority, little is definitive about their intricacies and impacts. Although data and research are helpful in understanding some of the aspects of stepfamilies, it's important to remember that each person and family is a unique entity.

For children, growing diversity in family living arrangements

% of children living with ...

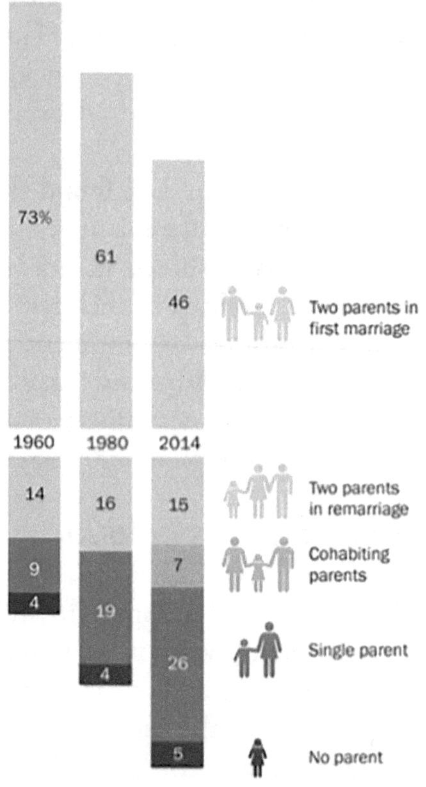

Note: Based on children under 18. Data regarding cohabitation are not available for 1960 and 1980; in those years, children with cohabiting parents are included in "one parent." For 2014, the total share of children living with two married parents is 62% after rounding. Figures do not add up to 100% due to rounding.

Source: Pew Research Center analysis of 1960 and 1980 decennial census and 2014 American Community Survey (IPUMS)

PEW RESEARCH CENTER

Family life is changing. Two-parent households are on the decline in the United States as divorce, remarriage and cohabitation are on the rise. And families are smaller now, both due to the growth of single-parent households and the drop in fertility. Not only are Americans having fewer children, but the circumstances surrounding parenthood have changed. While in the early 1960s babies typically arrived within a marriage, today fully four-in-ten births occur to women who are single or living with a non-marital partner. At the same time that family structures have transformed, so has the role of mothers in the workplace—and in the home. As more moms have entered the labor force, more have become breadwinners—in many cases, *primary* breadwinners—in their families.

As a result of these changes, there is no longer one dominant family form in the US Parents today are raising their children against a backdrop of increasingly diverse and, for many, constantly evolving family forms. By contrast, in 1960, the height of the post-World War II baby boom, there was one dominant family form. At that time 73% of all children were living in a family with two married parents in their first marriage. By 1980, 61% of children were living in this type of family, and today less than half (46%) are. The declining share of children living in what is often deemed a "traditional" family has been largely supplanted by the rising shares of children living with single or cohabiting parents.

Not only has the diversity in family living arrangements increased since the early 1960s, but so has the fluidity of the family. Non-marital cohabitation and divorce, along with the prevalence of remarriage and (non-marital) recoupling in the US, make for family structures that in many cases continue to evolve throughout a child's life. While in the past a child born to a married couple—as most children were—was very likely to grow up in a home with those two parents, this is much less common today, as a child's living arrangement changes with each adjustment in the relationship status of their parents. For example, one study found that over a three-year period, about three-in-ten (31%) children younger than 6 had experienced a major change in their family or household structure, in the form of parental divorce, separation, marriage, cohabitation or death.

Source: Kristin, "The American Family Today" (https://www.pewresearch.org/social-trends/2015/1 2/17/1-the-american-family-today/)

About the Author

Dr. Jeanette Moore ("Dr. Jeanette") was born and raised in Chicago, Illinois. She is a retiree who now resides in south suburban Chicago. Dr. Jeanette has adult children and grandchildren who reside in Illinois and Indiana. Dr. Jeanette has a love for God's word and enjoys teaching, reading, studying, and writing. She holds a doctorate degree in theological studies. *Blending a Family Successfully* is God breathed as it was put on her heart by God to write and to instruct others who have a desire to blend their families successfully, navigating through the challenges of life in keeping with the principles of God's word. Along with her God-given wisdom, Dr. Jeanette was able to share the experiences of fictitious characters of real-life challenges that embodied strength, character, and convictions of living a God-fearing life.